contents

introduction

section one: fruit juices

section two: vegetable juices

section three: **smoothies**

section four: **quenchers**

introduction

Savouring a home-made, fresh juice is – as anyone who has tried it will know – an immensely pleasurable experience. It tastes truly delicious, invigorates your body and mind, and gives the added satisfaction of having created it yourself.

Raw, fresh juice is also one of the most health-affirming, rejuvenating substances we can consume. It provides the body with nutrients on a superhighway, delivering within minutes easily digestible vitamins, minerals, carbohydrates and countless phytonutrients (nutrients derived from plants, which are increasingly being shown to boost health). These natural blends of nutrients work together to enhance immunity, helping to protect us from not just coughs and colds but cancer and cardiovascular disease.

Once you have developed the habit of making your own fresh juice combinations each morning, nothing else will do – a daily juice may soon become as natural and essential as brushing your teeth. Ahead of you are more recipes for juices, smoothies and quenchers than you could ever ask for. My breakfast is regularly a fresh, home-made juice and a creamy smoothie. You really couldn't get a better start to the day.

about the fan

This fan provides you with 101 recipes to guide and inspire you to begin a daily juicing habit. It is organized into chapters of juices, smoothies and quenchers. The difference between these can be explained as follows:

A juice is made by passing prepared fruits and vegetables through a special juice extractor or citrus press. This process extracts any fibre, but the resulting drink is very quickly digested and gives an immediate boost of energy.

A smoothie is made by mixing ingredients into a pulp in a blender. The result is a thicker drink, as it includes fruit and vegetable fibre – an important ingredient which helps to keep the guts moving and to maintain the right levels of good bacteria.

A quencher is an ultra-refreshing variation on a juice or smoothie which includes ingredients such as frozen fruit, ice or sparkling water.

Each recipe lists the main vitamins, minerals and other nutrients it contains. The specific health benefits of these nutrients are explained in a chart at the back of the fan. Each drink has also been given a star-rating, with marks out of five for its energy-boosting, detoxing and immunity-boosting properties, and for its benefits to the digestive system and the skin. Each recipe makes enough for two portions unless otherwise stated.

equipment you'll need

To make a variety of recipes, you will need a juice extractor, a citrus press and a blender, all of which can be found in most kitchen accessory shops or department stores and are available to suit a range of budgets. For the purposes of this fan, when I say "juice" a fruit, I mean put it into an electric juicer, and when I say "squeeze" a fruit, I mean extract its juice by squeezing on a citrus press.

storing juices and smoothies

You can't beat drinking juices or smoothies the moment you've made them. However, if you'd like to take them to work or on a picnic, prevent discoloration by putting a teaspoon of vitamin C powder or a squeeze of lemon in the jug before you juice. Also, keep the drink covered and cool.

choosing your ingredients

Where possible choose fresh, organic produce that is in season. Organic fruits and vegetables provide you with all the goodness you need and none of the agrochemicals you don't. For fruit juices, choose pieces that are almost but not quite ripe, as these yield the most juice and taste the best. Avoid juicing fruits that are over-ripe or too soft.

preparing your ingredients

FRUITS

APPLES: Wash well. For juicing, remove stalk and cut into pieces small enough to fit your juicer. For smoothies, core and chop.

APRICOTS (FRESH): Wash well. Halve and remove stone.

BANANAS: Can't be juiced. For smoothies, peel and break or slice into pieces.

BERRIES (BLACKBERRIES, BLACKCURRANTS, BLUEBERRIES, CRANBERRIES AND RASPBERRIES): Wash well. Pick out any that are mouldy or still attached to the hulls.

CHERRIES: Wash well. Slice in half and prise out stones or use an olive stoner.

DATES: Wash, halve and remove the pits.

GRAPEFRUIT: For juicing, peel and cut to fit. For squeezing, cut in half.

GRAPES: Wash well.

GUAVAS: Peel, halve, remove seeds and chop into chunks.

KIWIS: Peel and chop into chunks.

LEMONS AND LIMES: For juicing, peel and chop into chunks. For squeezing, cut in half.

MANGOES: Peel and slice flesh away from stone.

MELONS (CANTALOUPE/HONEYDEW): Halve, slice and cut flesh away from the rind. Chop flesh into chunks.

NECTARINES: Wash well. Halve, remove stone and chop into chunks.

ORANGES: For juicing, peel and chop into chunks. For squeezing, cut in half.

PAPAYA: Peel, remove seeds and chop into chunks.

PASSION FRUIT: Cut in half and scoop out flesh.

PEACHES: Wash well. Halve, remove stone and chop into chunks.

PEARS: Wash well. For juicing, remove stalk and cut to fit. For smoothies, core and chop.

PINEAPPLES: Chop off the top and bottom, and slice down the sides to remove the skin. For blending, remove any remaining eyes (there's no need if you are juicing).

STRAWBERRIES: Wash well. For blending, remove hulls (no need for juicing).

TANGERINES: For juicing, peel and chop into chunks. For squeezing, cut in half.

WATERMELONS: Slice out wedges and cut flesh away from the rind. Chop to fit.

VEGETABLES

BEET (BEETROOT): Top and tail, scrub well and cut to fit.

BROCCOLI: Wash well and cut to fit.

CABBAGE: Remove outer leaves and cut to fit.

CARROTS: Scrub well, top and tail, and cut to fit.

CELERY: Scrub well.

CUCUMBERS: Wash well and chop to fit.

GINGER: Wash well, peel and slice.

LETTUCE AND KALE: Wash leaves well.

PARSLEY: Wash well.

PARSNIPS: Scrub well, top and tail, and cut to fit.

SPINACH: Wash leaves well.

SWEET POTATOES: Scrub well and cut to fit.

TOMATOES: Wash well and slice to fit.

WATERCRESS: Wash well.

1   apple tropics

3 apples
$\frac{1}{2}$ pineapple
$\frac{1}{2}$ lime
$\frac{1}{2}$ passion fruit

An extra tang and a taste of the tropics are evident in this apple recipe. It's best to stir the passion fruit flesh into the juice once it's made, rather than passing it through the blender.

NUTRIENTS

Beta-carotene, folic acid, vitamin C; calcium, magnesium, manganese, phosphorus, potassium, sulphur

ENERGY	★★★★☆
DETOX	★★☆☆☆
IMMUNITY	★★★☆☆
DIGESTION	★★★★☆
SKIN	★★★☆☆

2 sweet c

3 apples
2 guavas

This is one of the few recipes for which I suggest using a sweeter variety of apple, such as Cox, to offset the tangy guava, which is a phenomenally rich source of vitamin C.

NUTRIENTS

Beta-carotene, folic acid, vitamin B3, vitamin C; calcium, magnesium, phosphorus, potassium, sodium, sulphur

ENERGY	★★★★☆
DETOX	★★★☆☆
IMMUNITY	★★★★★
DIGESTION	★☆☆☆☆
SKIN	★★★★☆

3 apple blush

3 apples
1 nectarine
8 strawberries

The delicate colour of this juice gives only
the slightest indication of its sensational
taste, especially if you use a tangy variety
of apple, such as Granny Smith, combined
with sweet, ripe strawberries.

NUTRIENTS

Beta-carotene, biotin, folic acid, vitamin C;
calcium, magnesium, phosphorus,
potassium, sulphur

ENERGY	★★★★★
DETOX	★★☆☆☆
IMMUNITY	★★★☆☆
DIGESTION	★☆☆☆☆
SKIN	★★★★☆

4 apple cleanser

2 apples
2 kale leaves
1 stick celery
$\frac{1}{3}$ long cucumber
$\frac{1}{2}$ beet (beetroot)

The fruitiness of the apples offsets the more challenging taste of the greens to produce this beautifully red detoxifying juice.

NUTRIENTS

Beta-carotene, folic acid, vitamin B3, vitamin C; calcium, iron, magnesium, manganese, phosphorus, potassium, sulphur

ENERGY	★★☆☆☆
DETOX	★★★★☆
IMMUNITY	★★★☆☆
DIGESTION	★★☆☆☆
SKIN	★★★☆☆

7 surprising sweetie

2 grapefruits
1 thick slice of melon
1 peach

You would never imagine that anything with grapefruit could be so sweet, let alone pack such an immune-boosting punch.

NUTRIENTS

Beta-carotene, folic acid, vitamin B3, vitamin C; calcium, magnesium, phosphorus, potassium, sodium, sulphur

ENERGY	★★★★☆
DETOX	★★☆☆☆
IMMUNITY	★★★★☆
DIGESTION	★★☆☆☆
SKIN	★★★★★

8 black grapefruit

2 grapefruits
1 handful blackberries
1 handful blackcurrants

A fabulous contrast of the colours as
they blend in the jug … and then a
fantastic boost to immunity. Best made
in summer with fresh berries.

NUTRIENTS

Beta-carotene, folic acid, vitamins B5, C and E;
calcium, iron, magnesium, manganese, phosphorus,
potassium, sodium, sulphur

ENERGY	★★★★☆
DETOX	★☆☆☆☆
IMMUNITY	★★★★★
DIGESTION	☆☆☆☆☆
SKIN	★★★★☆

9 florida blue

2 oranges
1 pink grapefruit
1 handful blueberries

If you use a sweet pink grapefruit, rather than a sharper white one, this blend is divine.

NUTRIENTS

Beta-carotene, biotin, folic acid, vitamins B1, B2, B6, C and E; calcium, magnesium, phosphorus, potassium, sodium, sulphur

ENERGY	★★★★☆
DETOX	★☆☆☆☆
IMMUNITY	★★★★★
DIGESTION	★★☆☆☆
SKIN	★★★☆☆

10 bright orange

2 oranges
4 carrots

The incredible colour of this simple combination heralds an equally amazing taste.

NUTRIENTS

Beta-carotene, folic acid, vitamin C; calcium, magnesium, phosphorus, potassium, sodium, sulphur

ENERGY	★★★★☆
DETOX	★★★☆☆
IMMUNITY	★★★★☆
DIGESTION	★☆☆☆☆
SKIN	★★★☆☆

11 power-packed c

3 oranges
1 guava
1 handful strawberries

With three of the richest sources of vitamin C mixed together, this is not only a delicious drink but is also a strong immune booster that helps to keep illnesses at bay.

NUTRIENTS

Beta-carotene, biotin, folic acid, vitamin B3, vitamin C; calcium, magnesium, phosphorus, potassium, sodium, sulphur

ENERGY	★★★★★
DETOX	★☆☆☆☆
IMMUNITY	★★★★★
DIGESTION	☆☆☆☆☆
SKIN	★★★★☆

12 orange crudités

2 oranges
½ long cucumber
2 carrots
1 stick celery

The three vegetables in this juice gently dilute the sweet, sharp taste of oranges, and make it a lighter, more refreshing drink.

NUTRIENTS

Beta-carotene, folic acid, vitamin C; calcium, magnesium, manganese, phosphorus, potassium, sodium, sulphur

ENERGY	★★★☆☆
DETOX	★★☆☆☆
IMMUNITY	★★★☆☆
DIGESTION	★★☆☆☆
SKIN	★★★☆☆

13 citrus sharp

3 oranges
1 lemon
1 lime

The colour of this refreshing juice hails a tart tickling of the tastebuds, and all that citrus fruit gives you a great immune boost.

NUTRIENTS

Beta-carotene, folic acid, vitamin C; calcium, magnesium, phosphorus, potassium, sodium, sulphur

ENERGY	★★★★☆
DETOX	★☆☆☆☆
IMMUNITY	★★★★★
DIGESTION	☆☆☆☆☆
SKIN	★★☆☆☆

14 orange winter crumble

2 oranges
2 apples
1 handful blackberries

I love the blend of orange juice with the traditional winter mixture of apple and blackberry used in pies and crumbles.

NUTRIENTS
Beta-carotene, folic acid, vitamin C, vitamin E; calcium, iron, magnesium, manganese, phosphorus, potassium, sodium, sulphur

ENERGY	★★★★★
DETOX	★★☆☆☆
IMMUNITY	★★★★★
DIGESTION	★☆☆☆☆
SKIN	★★★★☆

15 orange aniseed twist

3 oranges
2 sticks celery
$\frac{1}{4}$ fennel bulb

The fennel gives a great turn to this recipe, while the saltiness of the celery brings out the flavours. All in all, very refreshing.

NUTRIENTS

Beta-carotene, folic acid, vitamin C; calcium, magnesium, manganese, phosphorus, potassium, sodium, sulphur

ENERGY	★★★☆☆
DETOX	★☆☆☆☆
IMMUNITY	★☆☆☆☆
DIGESTION	★★★☆☆
SKIN	★☆☆☆☆

16 orange blush

3 oranges
1 apple
1 handful raspberries

A tangy pink juice which blends three fantastic fruits perfectly – definitely greater than the sum of its parts.

NUTRIENTS

Beta-carotene, biotin, folic acid, vitamin C; calcium, magnesium, manganese, phosphorus, potassium, sodium, sulphur

ENERGY	★★★★★
DETOX	★☆☆☆☆
IMMUNITY	★★★☆☆
DIGESTION	★☆☆☆☆
SKIN	★★★☆☆

17 raspberry sensation

2 large handfuls raspberries
$\frac{1}{2}$ pineapple

A truly sensational combination – go on,
spoil yourself with two independently
delicious fruits laden with goodness.

NUTRIENTS

Beta-carotene, biotin, folic acid, vitamin C; calcium,
magnesium, manganese, phosphorus, potassium,
sodium, sulphur

ENERGY	★★★★★
DETOX	★☆☆☆☆
IMMUNITY	★★☆☆☆
DIGESTION	★★★★☆
SKIN	★★★☆☆

18 creamy raspberry

2 large handfuls raspberries
$\frac{1}{2}$ melon
1 stick celery

With the creaminess of the melon, you'd think you were drinking more than just fruit juice, while the salty celery lifts all the flavours.

NUTRIENTS

Beta-carotene, biotin, folic acid, vitamin C; calcium, magnesium, manganese, phosphorus, potassium, sodium, sulphur

ENERGY	★★★★★
DETOX	★☆☆☆☆
IMMUNITY	★★★☆☆
DIGESTION	☆☆☆☆☆
SKIN	★★★★☆

19 gently raspberry

2 large handfuls raspberries
2 pears
$\frac{1}{4}$ cucumber

Not quite as strange a combination as you may initially think – the cucumber in this saves the pears from being drowned out by the raspberries.

NUTRIENTS

Beta-carotene, biotin, folic acid, vitamin C; calcium, magnesium, manganese, phosphorus, potassium, sodium, sulphur

ENERGY	★★★☆☆
DETOX	★☆☆☆☆
IMMUNITY	★★☆☆☆
DIGESTION	★☆☆☆☆
SKIN	★★☆☆☆

20 berry bonanza

2 large handfuls raspberries
1 handful blackcurrants
1 handful blueberries

Complete luxury … this berry combination is a blessing to your tastebuds and your body.

NUTRIENTS

Beta-carotene, biotin, folic acid, vitamins B1, B2, B5, B6, C and E; calcium, chromium, magnesium, phosphorus, potassium, sodium, sulphur

ENERGY	★★★★★
DETOX	★☆☆☆☆
IMMUNITY	★★★★★
DIGESTION	☆☆☆☆☆
SKIN	★★★★☆

21 minty peach

3 peaches or nectarines
1 apple
1 lime
1 small bunch fresh mint

Apple, lime and mint is one of the most refreshing combinations possible; here it's blended with the nectar of peaches.

NUTRIENTS

Beta-carotene, folic acid, vitamin B3, vitamin C; calcium, magnesium, phosphorus, potassium, sodium, sulphur

ENERGY	★★★★☆
DETOX	★☆☆☆☆
IMMUNITY	★★☆☆☆
DIGESTION	★★☆☆☆
SKIN	★★★★☆

22 pink peach

2 peaches or nectarines
1 handful strawberries
1 handful raspberries

A summer delight – each drop to be
savoured. Alter the berry combination
to change the flavour and the sweetness.

NUTRIENTS

Beta-carotene, biotin, folic acid, vitamin B3,
vitamin C; calcium, magnesium, phosphorus,
potassium, sodium, sulphur

ENERGY	★★★★★
DETOX	★★☆☆☆
IMMUNITY	★★★★☆
DIGESTION	★☆☆☆☆
SKIN	★★★★★

23 tangerine cream

3 peaches or nectarines
2 tangerines or clementines

Sometimes oranges simply won't do –
only the delicate taste of tangerines or
clementines. Combine them with peaches
or nectarines and you get a creamy,
sweet blend.

NUTRIENTS
Beta-carotene, folic acid, vitamin B3, vitamin C;
calcium, magnesium, phosphorus, potassium,
sodium, sulphur

ENERGY	★★★★★
DETOX	★☆☆☆☆
IMMUNITY	★★★★★
DIGESTION	★☆☆☆☆
SKIN	★★★★☆

24 sunset peach

2 peaches or nectarines
1 apple
2 carrots
1 handful raspberries

The carrots add a surprising creamy sweetness to this one and can even make up for getting a dud batch of raspberries which aren't that sweet.

NUTRIENTS

Beta-carotene, biotin, folic acid, vitamin B3, vitamin C; calcium, magnesium, manganese, phosphorus, potassium, sodium, sulphur

ENERGY	★★★★★
DETOX	★★☆☆☆
IMMUNITY	★★★★★
DIGESTION	★★☆☆☆
SKIN	★★★★☆

25 thicker than water

2 large handfuls cherries
2 apples
$\frac{1}{2}$ beet (beetroot)

The colour of this smooth, sumptuous juice almost makes you want to touch it as though it were soft, pink velvet.

NUTRIENTS

Beta-carotene, folic acid, vitamin C; calcium, magnesium, phosphorus, potassium, sodium, sulphur

ENERGY	★★★★★
DETOX	★★★☆☆
IMMUNITY	★★★★☆
DIGESTION	★★★☆☆
SKIN	★★★★☆

26 tropical pear

3 pears
$\frac{1}{4}$ pineapple
$\frac{1}{2}$ lime

Perhaps two of my favourite fruits with a hint of tangy lime.

NUTRIENTS

Beta-carotene, folic acid, vitamin C; calcium, magnesium, manganese, phosphorus, potassium, sodium, sulphur

ENERGY	★★★★☆
DETOX	★★☆☆☆
IMMUNITY	★★★★☆
DIGESTION	★★★☆☆
SKIN	★★☆☆☆

27 gut soother

2 pears
2 carrots
$\frac{1}{2}$ pineapple
$\frac{1}{2}$ inch (1 cm) ginger root

The blend of these three along with the ginger not only make a great taste, but they're good for the digestive tract too.

NUTRIENTS

Beta-carotene, folic acid, vitamin C; calcium, magnesium, manganese, phosphorus, potassium, sodium, sulphur

ENERGY	★★★☆☆
DETOX	★★☆☆☆
IMMUNITY	★★★☆☆
DIGESTION	★★★★★
SKIN	★★★☆☆

28 ginger zinger

$\frac{1}{2}$ pineapple
2 oranges
1 inch (2.5 cm) ginger root

One of the most refreshing, tangy combinations there is. You could add more ginger if you're a real fan and get an even greater boost from this all-round wonder food.

NUTRIENTS
Beta-carotene, folic acid, vitamin C; calcium, magnesium, manganese, phosphorus, potassium, sodium

ENERGY	★★★★☆
DETOX	★☆☆☆☆
IMMUNITY	★★★★☆
DIGESTION	★★★☆☆
SKIN	★★☆☆☆

29 muddy pine

1 pineapple
1 teaspoon spirulina powder

The tangy, strong taste of the pineapple
easily carries the earthy goodness of the
spirulina. Best to shake a bit of the juice
with the spirulina in a jar and then
mix it all up to avoid getting lumps of
green powder.

NUTRIENTS

Beta-carotene, folic acid, vitamins B1, B3, B5, B6
and C; calcium, iron, magnesium, manganese,
phosphorus, potassium, sodium

ENERGY   ★★★★★
DETOX   ★★★★★
IMMUNITY   ★★★☆☆
DIGESTION   ★★★★☆
SKIN   ★★★★☆

30 sweet sunset

$\frac{1}{2}$ pineapple
1 thick slice watermelon

The watery sweetness of the melon contrasts beautifully with the rich tang of pineapple in this all-round health-affirming, thirst-quenching drink.

NUTRIENTS

Beta-carotene, folic acid, vitamin B5, vitamin C; calcium, magnesium, manganese, phosphorus, potassium, sodium

ENERGY	★★★★★
DETOX	★★★☆☆
IMMUNITY	★★★★☆
DIGESTION	★★☆☆☆
SKIN	★★★★☆

31 digestaid

$\frac{1}{2}$ pineapple
1 thick slice white cabbage
1 inch (2.5 cm) ginger root
1 small bunch fresh mint

Pineapple contains bromelain (a natural substance that helps digestion), cabbage soothes the stomach lining and ginger calms the digestive tract – an all-round gut tonic.

NUTRIENTS

Beta-carotene, folic acid, vitamin C, vitamin E; calcium, magnesium, manganese, phosphorus, potassium, sodium

ENERGY	★★★☆☆
DETOX	★★★☆☆
IMMUNITY	★★☆☆☆
DIGESTION	★★★★★
SKIN	★★★☆☆

32 pineapple punch

2 pineapples
$\frac{1}{2}$ melon
8 guavas

This exquisite combination of fruits creates a creamy, magical taste and is packed with energy – the perfect alcohol-free alternative at any party. Makes 8 servings.

NUTRIENTS

Beta-carotene, folic acid, vitamin B3, vitamin C; calcium, magnesium, manganese, phosphorus, potassium, sodium, sulphur

ENERGY	★★★★★
DETOX	★★☆☆☆
IMMUNITY	★★★★★
DIGESTION	★★★☆☆
SKIN	★★★☆☆

33 easy morning

3 carrots
1 apple
$\frac{1}{2}$ orange
1 stick celery
$\frac{1}{2}$ inch (1 cm) ginger root

This is my absolute staple – when I'm not feeling any more adventurous, this is what pours daily from my juicer. It makes an invigorating start to any day.

NUTRIENTS

Beta-carotene, folic acid, vitamin C; calcium, magnesium, manganese, phosphorus, potassium, sodium, sulphur

ENERGY	★★★★☆
DETOX	★★★☆☆
IMMUNITY	★★★☆☆
DIGESTION	★★☆☆☆
SKIN	★★★☆☆

34 carrot cleanser

3 carrots
$\frac{1}{2}$ apple
$\frac{1}{2}$ orange
$\frac{1}{4}$ beet (beetroot)
1 stick celery
2 large kale leaves

Any juice using beet or kale can take some getting used to for the vegetable juice initiate, but once you've had it, you can fully appreciate its cleansing properties.

NUTRIENTS

Beta-carotene, folic acid, vitamins B3, B6 and C; calcium, iron, magnesium, manganese, phosphorus, potassium, sodium, sulphur

ENERGY	★★★☆☆
DETOX	★★★★★
IMMUNITY	★★★★☆
DIGESTION	★★★☆☆
SKIN	★★★☆☆

35 cold war

4 carrots
1 orange
$\frac{1}{2}$ inch (1 cm) ginger root
2 cloves garlic

The garlic in here is purely for therapeutic use – to give your immune system a powerful punch in the face of a cold or any other infection. It's a brave person who can stomach it on any normal morning, let alone the breath you're likely to have afterwards. To use, simply peel and slice before you add it to the juicer. If your chest is feeling congested, you could add half an onion.

NUTRIENTS

Beta-carotene, folic acid, vitamin C; calcium, magnesium, phosphorus, potassium, sodium, sulphur

ENERGY	★★★☆☆
DETOX	★★☆☆☆
IMMUNITY	★★★★★
DIGESTION	★★☆☆☆
SKIN	★★★★☆

36 veggie carotene catapult

3 carrots
1 red bell pepper
1 spear broccoli
$\frac{1}{2}$ sweet potato

Superbly rich in anti-aging and cancer-protective carotenes – and it tastes good.

NUTRIENTS

Beta-carotene, folic acid, vitamins B5, C and E; calcium, magnesium, phosphorus, potassium, sodium, sulphur

ENERGY	★★★★☆
DETOX	★★★☆☆
IMMUNITY	★★★★★
DIGESTION	★★★☆☆
SKIN	★★★★★

37 cool 'n' pale

1 cucumber
2 apples

A dreamy shade of green, with a taste
to match – this refreshing combination
of two highly juicy ingredients is very
cleansing on the palate.

NUTRIENTS

Beta-carotene, folic acid, vitamin C; calcium,
magnesium, phosphorus, potassium, sulphur

ENERGY   ★★★☆☆
DETOX   ★★★★☆
IMMUNITY   ★★☆☆☆
DIGESTION   ★★★☆☆
SKIN   ★★★☆☆

38 citrus cuke

1 cucumber
1 orange
1 grapefruit

Although the actual flavour of the cucumber gets a bit lost, its watery freshness transforms the orange and grapefruit into a more refreshing drink.

NUTRIENTS

Beta-carotene, folic acid, vitamin C; calcium, magnesium, phosphorus, potassium, sulphur

ENERGY	★★★★☆
DETOX	★★☆☆☆
IMMUNITY	★★★★☆
DIGESTION	☆☆☆☆☆
SKIN	★★★☆☆

39 tropical cucumber

1 cucumber
2 guavas
1 apple

The rich, tangy, tropical taste of guavas is toned down by the cucumber to form an unusual cooling juice.

NUTRIENTS

Beta-carotene, folic acid, vitamin B3, vitamin C; calcium, magnesium, phosphorus, potassium, sodium, sulphur

ENERGY	★★★★☆
DETOX	★★★★☆
IMMUNITY	★★★★☆
DIGESTION	★★☆☆☆
SKIN	★★★★☆

40 green waldorf

5 large kale leaves
2 apples
2 sticks celery
1 dessertspoon flaxseed
(linseed) oil

Well, not quite a Waldorf, but it tastes good and is super-healthy. The flax brings an unusual dimension in taste, texture and health properties to this cleansing juice.

NUTRIENTS

Beta-carotene, folic acid, vitamin B3, vitamin C; calcium, iron, magnesium, manganese, phosphorus, potassium, sodium, sulphur

ENERGY	★★★☆☆
DETOX	★★★★☆
IMMUNITY	★★★☆☆
DIGESTION	★★★★☆
SKIN	★★★★☆

41 hangover soother

1 bunch fresh parsley
1 handful watercress
4 broccoli spears
$\frac{1}{2}$ pineapple

Anything with pineapple in it is good in my book. This green goddess of a juice will refresh your palate, cleanse your system and have you back on your feet in no time.

NUTRIENTS

Beta-carotene, folic acid, vitamins B3, B5, C and E; calcium, iron, magnesium, phosphorus, potassium, sodium, sulphur

ENERGY	★★★☆☆
DETOX	★★★★★
IMMUNITY	★★☆☆☆
DIGESTION	★★★★☆
SKIN	★★★★☆

42 beetles

2 beets (beetroot)
2 apples
3 sticks celery

Another great combination of beet and
fruit, enhanced by the celery.

NUTRIENTS

Beta-carotene, folic acid, vitamin C; calcium,
magnesium, phosphorus, potassium,
sodium, sulphur

ENERGY	★★★★☆
DETOX	★★★★★
IMMUNITY	★★★☆☆
DIGESTION	★★★☆☆
SKIN	★★★★☆

43 carotene kick

1 sweet potato
$\frac{1}{2}$ melon
3 carrots

Sweet potatoes are a delicious, rich source of carotene, as are the other ingredients in this vibrant orange drink.

NUTRIENTS

Beta-carotene, folic acid, vitamin C, vitamin E; calcium, magnesium, phosphorus, potassium, sodium, sulphur

ENERGY	★★★★★
DETOX	★★★☆☆
IMMUNITY	★★★★★
DIGESTION	★★★☆☆
SKIN	★★★★★

44 tomato bell

6 tomatoes
2 bell peppers
1 stick celery
$\frac{1}{2}$ lemon
salt, pepper, Tabasco,
Worcestershire Sauce to taste

I'd only use red or yellow peppers for this as
the green ones tend to take over the other
flavours. Once you've juiced the vegetables
and lemon, season well, sit back and sip it
slowly, nibbling from a bowl of potato
chips, nuts and olives.

NUTRIENTS
Beta-carotene, biotin, folic acid, vitamin B3,
vitamin C, calcium, iron, magnesium, phosphorus,
potassium, sodium, sulphur

ENERGY	★★★★☆
DETOX	★★☆☆☆
IMMUNITY	★★★★☆
DIGESTION	☆☆☆☆☆
SKIN	★★★☆☆

vegetable juices

45 classic & green

6 tomatoes
3 carrots
1 large handful spinach

Classic tomato juice, but with an earthy, green undertone, this one is particularly good for the immune system as it's packed with carotenes.

NUTRIENTS

Beta-carotene, biotin, folic acid, vitamin B3, vitamin C; calcium, iron, magnesium, phosphorus, potassium, sodium, sulphur

ENERGY	★★★★☆
DETOX	★★★☆☆
IMMUNITY	★★★★★
DIGESTION	☆☆☆☆☆
SKIN	★★★★☆

46 classic combo

6 tomatoes
3 carrots
1 lime
1 small bunch mint

The two most popular and palatable of the
vegetable juices combined with a lift from
the mint and lime.

NUTRIENTS

Beta-carotene, biotin, folic acid, vitamin C;
calcium, magnesium, phosphorus, potassium,
sodium, sulphur

ENERGY	★★★★☆
DETOX	★★★☆☆
IMMUNITY	★★★★☆
DIGESTION	★☆☆☆☆
SKIN	★★★★☆

47 old favourites

4 tomatoes
1 orange
2 carrots

Three of the most popular individual juices rolled into one to create an interesting tasting juice that is great for your immunity.

NUTRIENTS

Beta-carotene, biotin, folic acid, vitamin C; calcium, magnesium, phosphorus, potassium, sodium, sulphur

ENERGY	★★★★☆
DETOX	★★☆☆☆
IMMUNITY	★★★★★
DIGESTION	☆☆☆☆☆
SKIN	★★★★☆

48 tomorange

4 tomatoes
2 oranges

One of the few combinations of tomato juice
and fruit that I think really works – very
refreshing and very good for you.

NUTRIENTS
Beta-carotene, biotin, folic acid, vitamin C;
calcium, magnesium, phosphorus, potassium,
sodium, sulphur

ENERGY	★★★★☆
DETOX	★★☆☆☆
IMMUNITY	★★★★★
DIGESTION	☆☆☆☆☆
SKIN	★★★☆☆

49 ginger tom

6 tomatoes
2 sticks celery
1 inch (2.5 cm) ginger root

Celery is probably my favourite juice to combine with tomatoes – the light saltiness takes the edge off the richer tomato – and the ginger in this one gives it all a sharp lift. You can be even more daring with the amount of ginger you use if you like.

NUTRIENTS

Beta-carotene, biotin, folic acid, vitamin C; calcium, magnesium, manganese, phosphorus, potassium, sodium, sulphur

ENERGY	★★★★☆
DETOX	★★☆☆☆
IMMUNITY	★★★★☆
DIGESTION	★☆☆☆☆
SKIN	★★★★☆

50 delicate pale

4 sticks celery
2 pears

Because pears tend to have a more delicate
flavour than apples, this juice has a subtle
taste but is very refreshing.

NUTRIENTS

Beta-carotene, folic acid, vitamin C; calcium,
magnesium, phosphorus, potassium,
sodium, sulphur

ENERGY	★★★☆☆
DETOX	★★★★☆
IMMUNITY	★★☆☆☆
DIGESTION	★★★☆☆
SKIN	★★☆☆☆

51 celery jointaid

3 sticks celery
$\frac{1}{2}$ pineapple
1 inch (2.5 cm) ginger root
1 dessertspoon flaxseed
(linseed) oil

With a combination of minerals, antioxidants and essential fats that helps to support healthy joints, this fresh juice also offers the anti-inflammatory properties of pineapple and ginger.

NUTRIENTS

Beta-carotene, folic acid, vitamin C; calcium, magnesium, manganese, phosphorus, potassium, sodium, sulphur

ENERGY	★★★★☆
DETOX	★★★★☆
IMMUNITY	★★★★★
DIGESTION	★★★★★
SKIN	★★★☆☆

52 pink punch

3 sticks celery
2 apples
1 handful cranberries
 (or raspberries)
3 sprigs fresh mint
$\frac{1}{2}$ inch (1 cm) ginger root

Who needs alcohol on a hot summer's day?

NUTRIENTS

Beta-carotene, folic acid, vitamin C; calcium, iron,
magnesium, manganese, phosphorus, potassium,
sodium, sulphur

ENERGY	★★★★☆
DETOX	★★★☆☆
IMMUNITY	★★★★☆
DIGESTION	★★☆☆☆
SKIN	★★☆☆☆

53 grape crunch

4 sticks celery
1 large bunch seedless grapes
(about 50)

There's something about the sweetness of
grapes that goes fantastically well with
celery. Use either green or red grapes,
although red are richer in antioxidants.

NUTRIENTS

Folic acid, vitamin C, vitamin E; calcium, manganese,
phosphorus, potassium, sodium, sulphur

ENERGY	★★★★☆
DETOX	★★★★☆
IMMUNITY	★★★☆☆
DIGESTION	★★☆☆☆
SKIN	★★★☆☆

54 soft and sharp

3 sticks celery
2 pears
1 large bunch watercress

The sharp contrast between the pear and the watercress goes well with the fresh, salty celery in this pretty, green drink.

NUTRIENTS

Beta-carotene, folic acid, vitamin C, vitamin E; calcium, iron, magnesium, phosphorus, potassium, sodium, sulphur

ENERGY	★★☆☆☆
DETOX	★★★★★
IMMUNITY	★★★★☆
DIGESTION	★★★☆☆
SKIN	★★★☆☆

55 chlorophyll crunch

3 sticks celery
3 carrots
1 bunch parsley

Creamy carrots, salty celery and perky parsley combine in this substantial drink that is a good detoxifier and all-round immune-boosting tonic. You really can taste the goodness.

NUTRIENTS

Beta-carotene, folic acid, vitamin B3, vitamin C; calcium, iron, magnesium, manganese, phosphorus, potassium, sodium, sulphur

ENERGY	★★☆☆☆
DETOX	★★★★★
IMMUNITY	★★★★★
DIGESTION	★★★☆☆
SKIN	★★★★☆

56 take heart

4 sticks celery
1 apple
1 handful blackcurrants
$\frac{1}{2}$ inch (1 cm) ginger root
1 dessertspoon flaxseed
   (linseed) oil

Each of the ingredients in this bright juice
has properties that can help to support
healthy blood pressure and blood vessels –
and it tastes great.

NUTRIENTS

Beta-carotene, biotin, folic acid, vitamin C,
vitamin E; calcium, magnesium, manganese,
phosphorus, potassium, sodium, sulphur

ENERGY	★★★☆☆
DETOX	★★★★☆
IMMUNITY	★★★★☆
DIGESTION	★★☆☆☆
SKIN	★★★★☆

57 veggie cocktail

3 sticks celery
3 tomatoes
2 carrots
$\frac{1}{2}$ lemon

A sweet, pale orange vegetable juice –
you could add some parsley too if you
want that green, cleansing taste.

NUTRIENTS

Beta-carotene, biotin, folic acid, vitamin C;
calcium, magnesium, manganese, phosphorus,
potassium, sodium, sulphur

ENERGY	★★★★☆
DETOX	★★★☆☆
IMMUNITY	★★★★★
DIGESTION	★☆☆☆☆
SKIN	★★★★☆

58 celery blood cleanser

3 sticks celery
1 apple
1 beet (beetroot)
1 teaspoon spirulina

You can hardly believe this is so good for you, it has such a fantastic taste. Put in a little less beet if you're not a hardened fan. Shake the spirulina with some of the juice in a jar before mixing in with the rest.

NUTRIENTS

Beta-carotene, folic acid, vitamins B1, B3, B5, B6 and C; calcium, iron, magnesium, manganese, phosphorus, potassium, sodium, sulphur

ENERGY	★★★☆☆
DETOX	★★★★★
IMMUNITY	★★★☆☆
DIGESTION	★★★★☆
SKIN	★★★★☆

59 black banana

- 2 bananas
- 2 heaped tablespoons blackcurrants
- 10 tablespoons (150 ml / $\frac{2}{3}$ cup) apple juice (or the juice from the blackcurrants, if they come from a can)

A wonderful contrast between the sweet banana and the tangy blackcurrants. Use blackcurrants canned in natural juice if you don't have fresh ones – a good standby to keep in the cupboard in winter.

NUTRIENTS

Beta-carotene, biotin, vitamins B1, B3, B6, C and E; calcium, iron, magnesium, phosphorus, potassium, sodium, sulphur

ENERGY	★★★★★
DETOX	★☆☆☆☆
IMMUNITY	★★★☆☆
DIGESTION	★☆☆☆☆
SKIN	★★★☆☆

60 pink lady

2 bananas
2 handfuls raspberries
10 tablespoons (150 ml / $\frac{2}{3}$ cup)
    cranberry juice

This one is certainly heaven-sent and gives
a great energy boost too.

NUTRIENTS

Beta-carotene, biotin, folic acid, vitamins B1, B3, B6
and C; calcium, iron, magnesium, manganese,
phosphorus, potassium, sodium, sulphur

ENERGY	★★★★★
DETOX	★☆☆☆☆
IMMUNITY	★★★☆☆
DIGESTION	★★☆☆☆
SKIN	★★★☆☆

61 banana pie

2 bananas
1 apple
1 handful blackberries
   (or blackcurrants)
10 tablespoons (150 ml / $\frac{2}{3}$ cup)
   apple juice

Not literally a pie, but I always think of the
apple and blackberry pie combination when
the two are blended. The sharpness cuts
deliciously through the dense flavour of
the banana.

NUTRIENTS

Beta-carotene, folic acid, vitamins B1, B3, B5, B6, C
and E; calcium, iron, magnesium, phosphorus,
potassium, sodium, sulphur

ENERGY   ★★★★★
DETOX   ★☆☆☆☆
IMMUNITY   ★★★☆☆
DIGESTION   ★★☆☆☆
SKIN   ★★☆☆☆

62 easy morning mash

2 bananas
1 pear
1 orange
8 tablespoons (120 ml / $\frac{1}{2}$ cup)
  apple juice

Just reach into the fruit bowl and whiz it all up. Easy.

NUTRIENTS

Beta-carotene, folic acid, vitamins B1, B3, B6 and C; calcium, magnesium, phosphorus, potassium, sulphur

ENERGY	★★★★★
DETOX	★☆☆☆☆
IMMUNITY	★★★☆☆
DIGESTION	★★☆☆☆
SKIN	★★☆☆☆

63 coconutty 'nana

2 bananas
$\frac{1}{2}$ pineapple
2 tablespoons (30 ml)
  coconut milk
8 tablespoons (120 ml / $\frac{1}{2}$ cup)
  pineapple juice

If you're a fan of coconut, you'll love this smoothie and the way it transports you to a warm, palm-fringed beach.

NUTRIENTS

Beta-carotene, folic acid, vitamins B1, B3, B6, C and E; calcium, magnesium, manganese, phosphorus, potassium, sodium, sulphur

ENERGY	★★★★★
DETOX	★☆☆☆☆
IMMUNITY	★★★☆☆
DIGESTION	★★★★☆
SKIN	★★☆☆☆

64 tropical treat

1 banana
$\frac{1}{2}$ pineapple
$\frac{1}{2}$ papaya
8 tablespoons (120 ml / $\frac{1}{2}$ cup)
guava juice

Fancy being transported to a fresh fruit salad on a beach in Thailand?

NUTRIENTS

Beta-carotene, folic acid, vitamin B3, vitamin C; calcium, magnesium, manganese, phosphorus, potassium, sodium, sulphur

ENERGY	★★★★★
DETOX	★☆☆☆☆
IMMUNITY	★★★☆☆
DIGESTION	★★★★☆
SKIN	★★★☆☆

65 creamy green banana

1 banana
$\frac{1}{4}$ pineapple
1 heaped teaspoon spirulina
5 tablespoons (75 ml / $\frac{1}{3}$ cup) natural yogurt
6 tablespoons (90 ml / $\frac{1}{2}$ cup) pineapple juice

This isn't to say you should use green bananas, but you turn a pale yellow smoothie into a pastel green by adding the spirulina.

NUTRIENTS

Beta-carotene, folic acid, vitamins B1, B3, B5, B6 and C; calcium, iron, magnesium, manganese, phosphorus, potassium, sodium, sulphur, zinc

ENERGY	★★★★☆
DETOX	★★★☆☆
IMMUNITY	★★★☆☆
DIGESTION	★★★★☆
SKIN	★★☆☆☆

66 creamy bananacot

2 bananas
4 apricots
5 tablespoons (75 ml / $\frac{1}{3}$ cup)
   natural yogurt
10 tablespoons (150 ml / $\frac{2}{3}$ cup)
   apricot or apple juice

When an apricot is ripe, it is food from the heavens. You can make this in winter with apricots canned in juice.

NUTRIENTS

Beta-carotene, folic acid, vitamins B1, B3, B5, B6 and C; calcium, magnesium, phosphorus, potassium, sulphur, zinc

ENERGY	★★★★☆
DETOX	☆☆☆☆☆
IMMUNITY	★★★☆☆
DIGESTION	★★★★☆
SKIN	★★★☆☆

67 banana heaven

2 bananas
4 dates (pitted)
1 teaspoon cocoa powder
$\frac{1}{2}$ teaspoon vanilla essence
1 teaspoon honey
1 teaspoon tahini
5 tablespoons (75 ml / $\frac{1}{3}$ cup)
   natural yogurt
10 tablespoons (150 ml / $\frac{2}{3}$ cup)
   pineapple juice

Unbelievably good, you'll wonder whether you're actually drinking a wickedly rich ice cream, laden with fat and calories.

NUTRIENTS

Beta-carotene, folic acid, vitamins B1, B3, B6 and C; calcium, magnesium, phosphorus, potassium, sulphur, zinc

ENERGY	★★★★★
DETOX	☆☆☆☆☆
IMMUNITY	★★★☆☆
DIGESTION	★★★☆☆
SKIN	★★★★☆

68 creamy passion

2 bananas
4 passion fruit
5 tablespoons (75 ml / $\frac{1}{3}$ cup)
   natural yogurt
10 tablespoons (150 ml / $\frac{2}{3}$ cup)
   guava juice

Surely one of the most exquisite
combinations of fruit ever, bound up with
creamy yogurt into a thick meal in itself.

NUTRIENTS

Beta-carotene, folic acid, vitamin B1, B3, B6 and C;
calcium, iron, magnesium, phosphorus, potassium,
sodium, sulphur

ENERGY	★★★★☆
DETOX	☆☆☆☆☆
IMMUNITY	★★★☆☆
DIGESTION	★★★☆☆
SKIN	★★☆☆☆

69 manilla

2 mangoes
4 tangerines
$\frac{1}{2}$ teaspoon vanilla essence
8 tablespoons (120 ml / $\frac{1}{2}$ cup)
 orange juice

A fruity smoothie made even sweeter with
the addition of vanilla

NUTRIENTS

Beta-carotene, folic acid, vitamin C, vitamin E;
calcium, iron, magnesium, phosphorus, potassium,
sodium, sulphur

ENERGY	★★★★★
DETOX	★☆☆☆☆
IMMUNITY	★★★★★
DIGESTION	★☆☆☆☆
SKIN	★★★☆☆

70 mango crush

2 mangoes
2 oranges
juice of a lime
8 tablespoons (120 ml / $\frac{1}{2}$ cup)
  apple juice

One pure orange colour, two different
tastes, one result – a fabulous smoothie
where the creamy, sweet mango
contrasts well with the tangy orange.

NUTRIENTS

Beta-carotene, folic acid, vitamin C, vitamin E;
calcium, iron, magnesium, phosphorus, potassium,
sodium, sulphur

ENERGY   ★★★★★
DETOX   ★☆☆☆☆
IMMUNITY   ★★★★★
DIGESTION   ★☆☆☆☆
SKIN   ★★★☆☆

71 mango blues

2 mangoes
2 handfuls blueberries
juice of a lime
8 tablespoons (120 ml / $\frac{1}{2}$ cup)
  apple juice

Tropic and temperate fruits
kicking up a storm in frothy red.

NUTRIENTS

Beta-carotene, biotin, folic acid, vitamins B1,
B2, B6, C and E; calcium, chromium, iron,
magnesium, phosphorus, potassium,
sodium, sulphur

ENERGY	★★★★★
DETOX	★★☆☆☆
IMMUNITY	★★★★★
DIGESTION	★★☆☆☆
SKIN	★★★★☆

72 mango zingo

2 mangoes
1 grapefruit
$\frac{1}{4}$ inch (0.5 cm) grated
    ginger root
8 tablespoons (120 ml / $\frac{1}{2}$ cup)
    apple juice

The slightly bitter grapefruit and spicy ginger blend beautifully with sweet, creamy mango to create this energy- and immunity-boosting drink.

NUTRIENTS

Beta-carotene, folic acid, vitamin C, vitamin E; calcium, iron, magnesium, phosphorus, potassium, sodium, sulphur

ENERGY	★★★★★
DETOX	★☆☆☆☆
IMMUNITY	★★★★★
DIGESTION	★★☆☆☆
SKIN	★★★☆☆

73 cocogo

2 mangoes
1 dessertspoon coconut milk
$\frac{1}{2}$ teaspoon vanilla essence
5 tablespoons (75 ml / $\frac{1}{3}$ cup)
natural yogurt
6 tablespoons (90 ml / $\frac{1}{2}$ cup)
pineapple juice

A sweet, creamy drink with the tropical
taste of coconut. Another one to transport
you to sunny climes.

NUTRIENTS

Beta-carotene, folic acid, vitamin C, vitamin E;
calcium, iron, magnesium, phosphorus, potassium,
sodium, sulphur, zinc

ENERGY	★★★★☆
DETOX	★☆☆☆☆
IMMUNITY	★★★★☆
DIGESTION	★★★☆☆
SKIN	★★★☆☆

74 berry mango

1 mango
1 handful strawberries
$\frac{1}{4}$ pineapple
5 tablespoons (75 ml / $\frac{1}{3}$ cup)
   natural yogurt
6 tablespoons (90 ml / $\frac{1}{2}$ cup)
   pineapple juice

The tangy pineapple contrasts
deliciously with the creamy
mango and sweet strawberries.

NUTRIENTS

Beta-carotene, folic acid, vitamin C,
vitamin E; calcium, iron, magnesium,
manganese, phosphorus, potassium,
sodium, sulphur, zinc

ENERGY   ★★★★☆
DETOX   ★☆☆☆☆
IMMUNITY   ★★★★☆
DIGESTION   ★★★★☆
SKIN   ★★★★☆

75 flecked mango

2 mangoes
2 handfuls blueberries
5 tablespoons (75 ml / $\frac{1}{3}$ cup)
  natural yogurt
8 tablespoons (120 ml / $\frac{1}{2}$ cup)
  apple juice

I love the flecks of blue that the skins of the
berries dot throughout this drink, let alone
the sublime taste they produce.

NUTRIENTS

Beta-carotene, biotin, folic acid, vitamins B1, B2, B6,
C and E; calcium, chromium, iron, magnesium,
phosphorus, potassium, sodium, sulphur, zinc

ENERGY	★★★★☆
DETOX	★☆☆☆☆
IMMUNITY	★★★★☆
DIGESTION	★★★☆☆
SKIN	★★★☆☆

76 pango mango

2 mangoes
2 peaches
$\frac{1}{2}$ teaspoon vanilla essence
5 tablespoons (75 ml / $\frac{1}{3}$ cup)
natural yogurt
8 tablespoons (120 ml / $\frac{1}{2}$ cup)
orange juice

Two fantastically tasty orange fruits taken to another realm with the hint of vanilla, which seems to make it even sweeter.

NUTRIENTS

Beta-carotene, folic acid, vitamins B3, C and E; calcium, iron, magnesium, phosphorus, potassium, sodium, sulphur, zinc

ENERGY	★★★★☆
DETOX	★☆☆☆☆
IMMUNITY	★★★★☆
DIGESTION	★★★☆☆
SKIN	★★★★☆

77 papaya salad

1 papaya
$\frac{1}{4}$ pineapple
1 slice watermelon
1 banana
8 tablespoons (120 ml / $\frac{1}{2}$ cup)
  pineapple juice

This combo of tropical fruits, a favourite among visitors to Thailand, is a delicious smoothie in any corner of the globe.

NUTRIENTS

Beta-carotene, folic acid, vitamins B1, B3, B5, B6 and C; calcium, magnesium, manganese, phosphorus, potassium, sodium, sulphur

ENERGY	★★★★★
DETOX	★★★☆☆
IMMUNITY	★★★★☆
DIGESTION	★★★★☆
SKIN	★★★★☆

78 heaven scent

1 papaya
1 grapefruit
1 handful raspberries
juice of a lime
8 tablespoons (120 ml / ½ cup)
grapefruit juice

Quite a magnificent combination of tastes.

NUTRIENTS

Beta-carotene, biotin, folic acid, vitamin C; calcium,
magnesium, manganese, phosphorus, potassium,
sodium, sulphur

ENERGY	★★★★★
DETOX	★☆☆☆☆
IMMUNITY	★★★★★
DIGESTION	★☆☆☆☆
SKIN	★★★★☆

79 creamy orange dream

3 peaches (or nectarines)
1 mango
1 orange
8 tablespoons (120 ml / $\frac{1}{2}$ cup)
   orange juice

Three different orange-coloured fruit, with
wonderfully contrasting tastes and textures.

NUTRIENTS

Beta-carotene, folic acid, vitamin B3,
vitamin C; calcium, iron, magnesium,
phosphorus, potassium, sodium, sulphur

ENERGY	★★★★★
DETOX	★☆☆☆☆
IMMUNITY	★★★★★
DIGESTION	★☆☆☆☆
SKIN	★★★★★

80 peach melba

3 peaches (or nectarines)
1 banana
1 handful raspberries
10 tablespoons (150 ml / $\frac{2}{3}$ cup)
    apple juice

An exquisite combination bursting with energy and taste.

NUTRIENTS

Beta-carotene, biotin, folic acid, vitamins B1, B3, B6 and C; calcium, magnesium, manganese, phosphorus, potassium, sodium, sulphur

ENERGY   ★★★★★
DETOX   ★☆☆☆☆
IMMUNITY   ★★★★☆
DIGESTION   ★★☆☆☆
SKIN   ★★★☆☆

smoothies

81 colour blend

2 peaches
1 banana
1 handful raspberries
5 tablespoons (75 ml / $\frac{1}{3}$ cup)
   natural yogurt
8 tablespoons (120 ml / $\frac{1}{2}$ cup)
   pineapple juice

Yellow and red make orange – here we have
all three. Best made in the summer with
juicy, ripe peaches and raspberries.

NUTRIENTS
Beta-carotene, biotin, folic acid, vitamins B1, B3, B6
and C; calcium, magnesium, phosphorus, potassium,
sodium, sulphur, zinc

ENERGY	★★★★☆
DETOX	★☆☆☆☆
IMMUNITY	★★★☆☆
DIGESTION	★★☆☆☆
SKIN	★★★★☆

82 apricot regular

8 rehydrated dried apricots
5 rehydrated prunes
5 tablespoons (75 ml / $\frac{1}{3}$ cup)
   natural yogurt
8 tablespoons (120 ml / $\frac{1}{2}$ cup)
   prune juice

Of course you can use any dried fruit, but apricots and prunes are particularly good and extremely rich in fibre and antioxidants. It's best to soak the fruit overnight before blending them.

NUTRIENTS

Beta-carotene, folic acid, vitamins B3, B5 and C; calcium, magnesium, phosphorus, potassium, sodium, sulphur, zinc

ENERGY	★★★★☆
DETOX	★☆☆☆☆
IMMUNITY	★★★★☆
DIGESTION	★★★★☆
SKIN	★★★★☆

83 sweet 'n' smooth

10 apricots
juice of half a lime
10 tablespoons (150 ml / $\frac{2}{3}$ cup)
    prune juice

The sweetness of these two combined is
fantastic, not to mention good for keeping
your guts going.

NUTRIENTS

Beta-carotene, folic acid, vitamins B3,
B5 and C; calcium, magnesium,
phosphorus, potassium, sulphur

ENERGY	★★★★★
DETOX	★☆☆☆☆
IMMUNITY	★★★★★
DIGESTION	★★★★★
SKIN	★★★★★

84 apricot zinger

5 apricots
2 pears
$\frac{1}{4}$ inch (0.5 cm) grated
ginger root
10 tablespoons (150 ml / $\frac{2}{3}$ cup)
apple juice

A surprising combination that blends
beautifully thanks to the hot ginger
contrasting with the rich, sweeter apricots.

NUTRIENTS

Beta-carotene, folic acid, vitamins B3, B5 and C;
calcium, magnesium, phosphorus,
potassium, sulphur

ENERGY	★★★★★
DETOX	★☆☆☆☆
IMMUNITY	★★★★★
DIGESTION	★★★☆☆
SKIN	★★★★★

85 creamy berry tang

2 handfuls strawberries
2 handfuls raspberries
2 oranges
5 tablespoons (75 ml / $\frac{1}{3}$ cup)
   natural yogurt
6 tablespoons (90 ml / $\frac{1}{2}$ cup)
   guava juice

The guava juice really brings out the flavours in this one.

NUTRIENTS

Beta-carotene, biotin, folic acid, vitamin B3, vitamin C; calcium, magnesium, manganese, phosphorus, potassium, sodium, sulphur

ENERGY	★★★★☆
DETOX	★☆☆☆☆
IMMUNITY	★★★★☆
DIGESTION	★★☆☆☆
SKIN	★★★★☆

86 pink melon

2 handfuls strawberries
$\frac{1}{2}$ melon
5 tablespoons (75 ml / $\frac{1}{3}$ cup)
    natural yogurt
6 tablespoons (90 ml / $\frac{1}{2}$ cup)
    apple juice

Even though I don't normally like melon with yogurt, this blend is fantastic.

NUTRIENTS

Beta-carotene, biotin, folic acid, vitamin C;
calcium, magnesium, phosphorus, potassium,
sodium, sulphur

ENERGY	★★★★☆
DETOX	★☆☆☆☆
IMMUNITY	★★★★☆
DIGESTION	★★★☆☆
SKIN	★★★★☆

smoothies

87 mango in disguise

3 handfuls blueberries and
   blackberries
1 mango (or 2!)
5 tablespoons (75 ml / $\frac{1}{3}$ cup)
   natural yogurt
6 tablespoons (90 ml / $\frac{1}{2}$ cup)
   guava juice

You can barely discern the mango from the
colour, but its taste reminds you it's there.
The guava adds another dimension altogether.

NUTRIENTS
Beta-carotene, biotin, folic acid, vitamins B1, B2, B6,
C and E; calcium, chromium, iron, magnesium,
manganese, phosphorus, potassium, sodium,
sulphur, zinc

ENERGY   ★★★★☆
DETOX   ★☆☆☆☆
IMMUNITY   ★★★★☆
DIGESTION   ★★★☆☆
SKIN   ★★★★☆

88 mighty berry

4 handfuls blueberries,
blackberries, blackcurrants,
strawberries, raspberries
5 tablespoons (75 ml / $\frac{1}{3}$ cup)
natural yogurt
6 tablespoons (90 ml / $\frac{1}{2}$ cup)
cranberry juice

Get them all in, any black, blue or red you
can get your hands on, for a powerful
taste sensation, not to mention a glassful
of goodness.

NUTRIENTS

Beta-carotene, biotin, folic acid, vitamins B1, B2, B5,
B6, C and E; calcium, chromium, iron, magnesium,
manganese, phosphorus, potassium, sodium,
sulphur, zinc

ENERGY	★★★★☆
DETOX	★★☆☆☆
IMMUNITY	★★★★☆
DIGESTION	★★★☆☆
SKIN	★★★★☆

89 pastel perfect

$\frac{1}{2}$ pineapple
3 kiwi fruits
8 tablespoons (120 ml / $\frac{1}{2}$ cup)
   pineapple juice

A delicious mix that can be sharp on the
tongue if the fruits aren't nice and ripe,
so pick your moment well.

NUTRIENTS

Beta-carotene, folic acid, vitamin C; calcium,
magnesium, manganese, phosphorus,
potassium, sodium

ENERGY	★★★★★
DETOX	★★☆☆☆
IMMUNITY	★★★★☆
DIGESTION	★★★☆☆
SKIN	★★★☆☆

90 pineberry

$\frac{1}{2}$ pineapple
1 handful cranberries
1 handful strawberries
8 tablespoons (120 ml / $\frac{1}{2}$ cup)
   pineapple juice

The sharp taste of the cranberries in this smoothie is well balanced by the sweetness of all the other ingredients.

NUTRIENTS

Beta-carotene, biotin, folic acid, vitamin C; calcium, iron, magnesium, manganese, phosphorus, potassium, sodium, sulphur

ENERGY	★★★★★
DETOX	★★☆☆☆
IMMUNITY	★★★★☆
DIGESTION	★★☆☆☆
SKIN	★★★☆☆

91 passionate pine

$\frac{1}{2}$ pineapple
$\frac{1}{2}$ banana
2 passion fruit
5 tablespoons (75 ml / $\frac{1}{3}$ cup)
   natural yogurt
8 tablespoons (120 ml / $\frac{1}{2}$ cup)
   pineapple juice

Almost anything with passion fruit is a hit for me and this is definitely no exception.

NUTRIENTS

Beta-carotene, folic acid, vitamins B1, B3, B6 and C; calcium, magnesium, manganese, phosphorus, potassium, sodium, sulphur, zinc

ENERGY	★★★★☆
DETOX	★☆☆☆☆
IMMUNITY	★★☆☆☆
DIGESTION	★★★★☆
SKIN	★☆☆☆☆

92 watermelon crush

$\frac{1}{2}$ small watermelon
  (or 2 thick slices)
2 handfuls raspberries

A tantalizing tastebud sensation, and as for the colour …

NUTRIENTS

Beta-carotene, biotin, folic acid, vitamin B5, vitamin C; calcium, magnesium, manganese, phosphorus, potassium, sodium, sulphur

ENERGY	★★★★★
DETOX	★★☆☆☆
IMMUNITY	★★★★★
DIGESTION	★☆☆☆☆
SKIN	★★★★★

93 paw paw sharp

$\frac{1}{2}$ paw paw (papaya)
2 scoops lime sorbet
a few dashes of mineral water

I just love the Australian name for papaya –
paw paw – and this drink certainly does it
justice. Just drop all the ingredients into
the blender and mix for about a minute.

NUTRIENTS

Beta-carotene, folic acid, vitamin C; calcium,
magnesium, phosphorus, potassium,
sodium, sulphur

ENERGY	★★★★★
DETOX	★☆☆☆☆
IMMUNITY	★★★★☆
DIGESTION	★★★★☆
SKIN	★★★☆☆

94 mango squeeze

2 grapefruits, juiced
2 mangoes
6 ice cubes

Mango is perfect for toning down the
tanginess of the grapefruit – all in all super
refreshing and a sweet but uplifting blend.
Drop all the ingredients into the blender
and mix for about a minute.

NUTRIENTS

Beta-carotene, folic acid, vitamin C, vitamin E;
calcium, iron, magnesium, phosphorus, potassium,
sodium, sulphur

ENERGY	★★★★★
DETOX	★☆☆☆☆
IMMUNITY	★★★★★
DIGESTION	★★☆☆☆
SKIN	★★★★☆

quenchers

95 double red creamy

2 handfuls frozen strawberries
2 handfuls frozen raspberries
2 tablespoons natural yogurt
a few dashes cranberry juice

Tangy, sweet and creamy all at once, this bright red freezie is exquisite. Just drop everything in the blender and mix for about a minute.

NUTRIENTS

Beta-carotene, biotin, folic acid, vitamin B12, vitamin C; calcium, iron, magnesium, manganese, phosphorus, potassium, sodium, sulphur, zinc

ENERGY	★★★★☆
DETOX	★☆☆☆☆
IMMUNITY	★★★☆☆
DIGESTION	★★☆☆☆
SKIN	★★★☆☆

96 strawberries on sunbeds

$\frac{1}{2}$ pineapple, frozen in chunks
1 handful frozen strawberries
1 tablespoon (15 ml)
 coconut milk
a few dashes of
 pineapple juice

Sit back and relax – you'd be forgiven for wondering where in the world you are with this sublime mix. Just pop everything in the blender and mix for a minute.

NUTRIENTS

Beta-carotene, biotin, folic acid, vitamin C; calcium, magnesium, manganese, phosphorus, potassium, sodium, sulphur

ENERGY	★★★★★
DETOX	★☆☆☆☆
IMMUNITY	★★★★☆
DIGESTION	★★☆☆☆
SKIN	★★★☆☆

97 fizzy berry crush

2 handfuls strawberries
2 handfuls blueberries
4–6 ice cubes
sparkling mineral water to top up

First blend the strawberries and blueberries
with the ice, then top up the jug with
water, so you get a fantastic texture as
well as taste.

NUTRIENTS

Beta-carotene, biotin, folic acid, vitamins B1, B2, B6,
C and E; calcium, chromium, magnesium,
phosphorus, potassium, sodium, sulphur

ENERGY ★★★★☆
DETOX ★★★☆☆
IMMUNITY ★★★★★
DIGESTION ☆☆☆☆☆
SKIN ★★★★☆

98 kiwi melon

$\frac{1}{2}$ melon
2 kiwi fruits
juice of a lime
4–6 ice cubes
sparkling mineral water to top up

Another blended fizzie – pulp the melon,
kiwi, lime juice and ice before topping up
with the mineral water for a delicious
summery cocktail.

NUTRIENTS

Beta-carotene, folic acid, vitamin C; calcium,
magnesium, phosphorus, potassium,
sodium, sulphur

ENERGY	★★★★☆
DETOX	★★★☆☆
IMMUNITY	★★★★★
DIGESTION	★☆☆☆☆
SKIN	★★★★☆

99 apple spice

$\frac{1}{2}$ inch (1 cm) grated or finely
  sliced ginger root
2 cinnamon sticks
7 fl oz (200 ml / $\frac{3}{4}$ cup) water
1 teaspoon honey
4 tablespoons (60 ml / $\frac{1}{4}$ cup)
  frozen stewed apple
7 fl oz (200 ml / $\frac{3}{4}$ cup) apple juice

This is a deliciously summery blend of
apples and spices. Alternatively, you could
drink it warm on a cold winter's night.

Bring the water, ginger and cinnamon to the boil
and leave to simmer for at least five minutes. Strain,
add the honey and leave to cool. Meanwhile, mix
the apple and apple juice in a blender and gradually
add the cooled tea.

100 fresh sensation

1 small bunch fresh mint leaves
1 inch (2.5 cm) grated ginger root
9 fl oz (300 ml / $1\frac{1}{4}$ cups) water
4 oranges, freshly juiced
1 scoop lime sorbet
4–6 ice cubes

A combination of refreshing, tangy ingredients to cool down on a summer's day.

Pour boiling water over the leaves and grated ginger, steep for five minutes. Leave to cool, top up with freshly squeezed orange juice, lime sorbet and ice.

101 spicy peachy cream

4 cardamom pods
2 cinnamon sticks
7 fl oz (200 ml) water
3 peaches, frozen in chunks
$\frac{1}{2}$ teaspoon vanilla essence
3 tablespoons (45 ml)
  natural yogurt
3–5 ice cubes

This one is almost a dessert in itself – a fantastic blend of eastern spices, fresh peaches and creamy yogurt.

Bring the water, cardamom and cinnamon to the boil and leave to simmer for at least five minutes. Strain and leave to cool. Meanwhile mix the peaches, vanilla and yogurt in a blender and gradually add the spice tea. Top with ice cubes and sip slowly through a straw.

NUTRIENT CHART

VITAMINS

Vitamin A: Antioxidant. Keeps skin and vision healthy. Anti-cancer.

Beta-carotene: Plant form of vitamin A. Antioxidant. Protects skin.

Vitamin B1: Aids metabolism, growth and development. Maintains nerves and muscles.

Vitamin B2: Helps to release energy from food. Maintains healthy nerves and skin.

Vitamin B3: Helps to maintain optimum energy levels. Keeps nervous system, digestive system and skin healthy.

Vitamin B5: Helps the body's response to stress. Aids antibody production and cell regeneration.

Vitamin B6: Promotes a healthy nervous system, brain and mental state.

Vitamin B12: Maintains the health of the blood, bone marrow, brain and nervous system.

Biotin: Needed for healthy skin, nails and hair. Aids fat metabolism.

Folic acid: Helps red blood cell production and development of a healthy nervous system.

Vitamin C: Antioxidant. Aids iron absorption and wound-healing. Helps to protect against cancer, heart disease, allergies, infections, colds, stress and even ageing.

Vitamin E: Antioxidant. Good for blood cells, muscles and nervous system. Protects against heart disease and some cancers.

Vitamin K: Ensures normal blood clotting.

MINERALS

Calcium: Builds healthy bones and teeth. Maintains heart, nerve and muscle tissues.

Chromium: Helps to balance blood sugar levels, so aids energy and concentration.

Iodine: Helps to control metabolism.

Iron: Enables oxygen transport. Maintains energy. Supports nerves and liver function.

Magnesium: Maintains bones and teeth. Helps energy production.

Manganese: Helps to keep nerves, brain and cells healthy. Aids fat metabolism.

Phosphorus: Aids energy production. Helps to build bones and teeth.

Potassium: Keeps heart, muscles and nerves healthy. Boosts energy and strength.

Selenium: Antioxidant. Helps to protect against heart disease and some cancers.

Sodium: Helps to control water balance. Regulates nerve and muscle function.

Sulphur: Antioxidant. Helps liver function. Keeps skin healthy.

Zinc: Antioxidant. Maintains skin health. Maintains healthy reproductive organs.